The Dedalus Press

Winter on White Paper

Elisabeth Borchers

translated from German by **Eva Bourke**

Poetry Europe 12

WINTER AUF WEISSEM BLATT

WINTER ON WHITE PAPER

ELISABETH BORCHERS

translated by

EVA BOURKE

DEDALUS

The Dedalus Press
24 The Heath, Cypress Downs, Dublin 6W
Ireland

ISBN 1 901233 83 9

The publisher acknowledges the financial assistance of
Ireland Literature Exchange (Translation Fund), Dublin Ireland.
www.irelandliterature.com
info@irelandliterature.com

Dedalus Press books are distributed in the U.K. by
Central Books, Ltd. 99 Wallis Road, London E9 5LN,
and in the U.S.A. and Canada by
Dufour Editions Inc., PO Box 7, Chester Springs,
Pennsylvania 19425 – 0007

The Dedalus Press receives financial assistance from An Chom-
hairle Ealaíon, The Arts Council, Ireland

Printed by Johnswood Press, Dublin

Introduction

On reading Elisabeth Borchers' poems the words that come to mind are wisdom, erudition, simplicity and serenity. Considering the bare facts of her biography — she was born in 1926, the daughter of a French mother and a German father, grew up in the Alsace, lost her father in 1946, married, had two sons, divorced, lived for a time in the United States and on returning to Germany became literary editor for two renowned publishing houses, most notably Suhrkamp in Frankfurt, a position she held until very recently — it quickly becomes clear, how hard-won these qualities are. Her life spans some of the most traumatic years in European history. When she was barely twenty she was confronted with the complete devastation of a culture and language. Like her literary contemporaries she believed that the only way to cleanse the German language of the corruption effected by Nazi propaganda was to keep the poem clear, undecorated and almost minimalist. From her early collections on to the three recent ones, "Who Lives" (1986), "On the Grammar of the Present Day" (1992) and "What is the Answer" (1998), from which this selection is taken, her poems' brevity and laconic sparseness give witness to this.

Lucidity of style, however, must not be confused with simplicity of meaning, or playfulness and the use of elements from fairytale or children's songs with optimism. The price the poet had to pay for her lightness of touch, her brilliant flashes of irony, is high. There is a dark undercurrent running through all the poems, of yearning and of loss; for instance, loss of loved ones, friends, home. Where is home, she asks, is it "between Orion and Eos / 460 parsec away and lost in a nebula"?

"Heimat" (Home), a most longed-for thing, is given mystical, almost religious dimensions — it is lost in the cosmos or with the dead, it is a dream or a memory but nowhere can it be found in the present which only signifies war. Hope lies in a distant transcendental future: "Home is a short sentence / a long sentence a verse / a word an Amen". As the poet had to accept her unhousedness in this world, so, too, must she accept the fact that although

5

the shepherd boy in the painting by Lenbach — "my painting I never owned" — has survived two world wars and is triumphant, the blue sky above his reclining figure is as terrifyingly vast and "answerless" today as it was to the small girl scrutinizing it in her uncle's study.

The poet's search for an answer is expressed in her persistent questioning. Her collection of 1998 is entitled "What is the Answer", but it is not only the answers that elude her but sometimes also perplexingly the questions: "What is the answer / what is the question", she asks herself contemplating the mystery of a small stele by Robert Stern, a visitation from "the land of silence / where pharaohs rest."

Perhaps it is the land of silence which is the poet's true home. Her poems are often epigrammatically brief, enigmatic and leave much unsaid, yet paradoxically an important motif in Borchers' work is language itself. Grammatical terms like present, past, noun, verb or syntax abound. She recalls the present moment granted to the poet "before the ordering of tenses" as a time of lavishness. In opposition to clinical grammatical order stands poetry which is invested with redemptive power. "Script", for instance, with all its variations of meaning, from "handwriting" to "manuscript" to "the scriptures", "word", "text", "alphabet", "the Holy Letters" — all these appear again and again as symbols of truth, clarity and deliverance or are sometimes perceived as a life-giving force in which the poet — not without irony — places her trust: "...and [I] ask the Holy Letters / to prolong my life. // As has repeatedly happened."

The angel the poet has chosen among the many "golden ones", the " hyphen of my nouns", the indispensable constituent of her every word, represents the transcendental element in her poetry, giving it meaning despite the sorrow "growing darker and darker" in his eyes.

Eva Bourke

Contents

Alles ist immer schon viele Jahre her

auch gestern und heute und morgen
und du und ich
die Lebenden und die Toten.
Wie das Wort das ich gegeben und genommen habe
wie der verspätete Zug, das Schlaflied, die Pflaumenbäume
das Grün von Zedern und Reben
grüner als das Grünzeug der Hoffnung
heller als die Lichter jenseits der Grenze.
Schwärzer als der Sturz ins Schwarz
fahren wir dahin wie ein Schatten, ein Schlitten.
Jung wie die Jugend von Joseph Conrad.
Das bricht mir das zerbrochene Nerz.
Und nach vielen Jahren verlasse ich den Ort mit diesem Gedicht.

Étonne-moi
Sagte Cocteau

Und Picasso
malte ein neues Gesicht
mit einem neuen Auge
in einer neuen Stirn
und vergaß, was es sonst noch gibt
auf dieser Welt

Und Chagall
malte drei Teller
voll Erdbeeren
und die Welt wurde nicht satt

Everything is always many years ago

also yesterday and today and tomorrow
and you and I
the living and the dead.
like the word I gave and took
like the train arriving too late, the lullabye, the plumtrees
the green of cedars and vines
greener than the greenery of hope
brighter than the lights beyond the border.
Blacker than the fall into blackness
we coast along like a shadow, a sledge.
Young like the youth of Joseph Conrad.
That's breaking my broken heart.
And after many years I leave the place with this poem.

Étonne-moi
Said Cocteau

And Picasso painted a new face
with a new eye
in a new forehead
and forgot everything else that exists
in this world

And Chagall
painted three plates
full of strawberries
and the world could not get enough

Erleuchtung

Seit Tagen schon ist der Strauß verwelkt
Ungeschält liegt der Spargel
Ein Korb voll Wäsche
Ungelesen das Manuskript von M & D
Die Zeitungen
Die Briefe
Seidiger Staub
Aufruhr im Baum vor dem Fenster

Essenszeit. Ausgehzeit. Schlafenszeit.

Ich, Gedichte lesend, lese
Die Sonne lasse sich auf seinem Kopf nieder
Welch eine Ehrung
Mich zu erleuchten.

Schade Sehr Schade

wie der Regen fällt und versinkt
wie auch das Licht
fällt und versinkt.

Sehr schade.

Und die Straße macht einen Knick
daß du entschwindest
fällst und versinkst
wie ein gestern gehörtes
unbegriffenes Wort.

Illumination

For days now the flowers are wilted
The asparagus lies unpeeled
A basket full of laundry
The manuscript by M & D unread
The newspapers
The letters
Silken dust
Riots in the tree outside the window

Dinnertime. Going-out time. Bedtime.

Reading poems, I read
That the sun alights on his head
What an honour
To illuminate me.

Pity. A Great Pity

how rain falls and sinks
how also the light
falls and sinks.

A great pity.

And the road makes a sharp bend
so that you vanish
fall and sink
like a word heard yesterday
and not grasped.

Trompe l'oeil
Oder Eine Zusammenfassung der Abschiede

Da stehst du ja immer noch
am Ufer des Sees rufe ich
zum See hinunter dorthin
wo die Zypressen stehn
obwohl ich vor Jahren dich
über die Berge gehn sah
durch tiefes tiefes Tal
flüchtig wie Abendlicht.

Und nun stehst du immer noch da
schattenwerfend wie die Zypresse
einbeinig
still wie Gestein
verläßlich wie die Gezeiten.

Daß ich nicht lache
nicht weine.

Winter
auf weissem Blatt, Zweihundertjährig

Und der Schnee verschneit
auch das Alphabet.
Welch eine ohne das zugeschneite Alphabet
nicht zu beschreibende Reinheit
in Erwartung der Schrift.

Trompe l'oeil
or A Summary of the Farewells

You are still standing there
on the lakeshore I call
down to the lake to
where the cypresses stand
although I saw you years ago
walk across the mountains
through deep deep valley
fleeting as evening light.

And you are still standing there now
casting a shadow like the cypress
one-legged
still as stone
reliable as the tides.

It's enough to make me laugh
or cry.

Winter
on Two Hundred Year-old Paper

And the snow buries
even the alphabet.
Such purity in anticipation of script
cannot be described
without the snow-covered alphabet.

Beweis

Aufgestanden um drei
Die Räume erleuchtet
Gefrühstückt
Und der Welt bewiesen
Noch bin ich ein wenig
Mein Herr.

Engel auf dem Schlossaltar von T.

Unter allen Goldenen
habe ich dich erwählt
mit dem Füllhorn
dem geschürzten Gewand
überm Knie.
Bindestrich
meiner Hauptwörter.
Ich habe dich erwählt
versehen mit Schloß
und mit Riegel.
Ungeachtet der immer
dunkler werdenden
Betrübnis deiner Augen.

Proof

Rose at three
Lit up the rooms
Had breakfast
And proved to the world
That to some small extent
I'm still my own master.

Angel on the Altar of the Castle at T.

Among all the golden ones
I have chosen you
with the cornucopia
the garment gathered
above your knee.
Hyphen
of my nouns.
I have chosen you
supplied with lock
and with key.
Regardless of the sorrow
growing darker and darker
in your eyes.

Allmächtig

Ich werde dich erfinden
ohne Maß und Ziel.
Wie Kreislauf läuft.
Und herrenlos wie Hund und Gras
nehm ich dich an.

Ich will dich mir verheißen
wie den Blick des ungebrochnen Lichts.

Ich werde dich an mich vergeuden
im Präsens, das vor der Regelung der Zeiten
mir zugesprochen worden ist.

Ich werde dich mir einverleiben
wie Jahre ineinander übergehen
ganz ohne Übergang.

Ich schreibe dich.
Das ist Allmacht.
Ist das Jetzt.

Omnipotent

I will invent you
without measure and purpose.
The way blood circulates.
And masterless as dog and grass
I accept you.

I want to pledge you to myself
like the gaze of unbroken light.

I will squander you on myself
in the present granted to me
before the ordering of tenses.

I will absorb you into myself
as years run into each other
quite without transition.

I write you.
That is omnipotence.
Is the Now.

Nächstenliebe

Ich liebe meinen Nächsten wie mich selbst.
Er ist mir nah wie Himmel,
Erde, Hut und Schuh.
Wie Kopf und Hand sich nahe sind.
Wie Bach und Stein.

Ich bin so nah, daß sich das Eisen spannt.
Und es schlägt zu, wie Hagelschlag.
Es schmerzt wie Schmerz,
der wie Musik zu hoch
zu tief gerät.

Herbst

Es stürzen Blatt um Blatt
Und jedes Blatt stürzt
sich zu Tode

*

Ich bewege mich auf den Park zu.
Der Park kommt mir nicht mehr entgegen.
Er geht zu Ende.
Wie ein Roman.

Neighbourly Love

I love my neighbour as myself.
He is close to me as sky,
earth, hat and shoe.
As head and hand are close.
As stream and stone.

I am so close that the iron strains.
And it strikes down as a hail storm
It pains like pain
which like music
ends up too high
too low.

Autumn

Leaf after leaf plummets down
And each leaf hurls
itself to death

*

I make my way towards the park.
The park no longer comes to meet me.
It is nearing its end.
Like a novel.

Ruhe

Wenn alles zur Ruhe kommt
und die Ruhe ist mächtig
wie die Rundung der Erde
Wenn alles zur Ruhe kommt

Grund und Boden
Baum und Strauch
Explosion und Implosion
Konzept und Ausführung

Wenn ich in Frieden gehe
und mein Fuß stößt
an keinen Stein

nehme ich wahr das Flimmern
das Blaulicht der Hortensien
und rufe um Hilfe.

Die Kunst der Überredung

Es grünen Stock und Stein
Sodom wird blühen
Gomorrha wird leuchten.

Stillness

When all becomes still
and the stillness is as powerful
as the curve of the earth
When all becomes still

Ground and land
tree and shrub
explosion and implosion
concept and realization

When I walk in peace
and my foot does not
stumble over a stone

I notice the hydrangeas
flashing their blue lights
and call for help.

The Art of Persuasion

Stick and stone are in leaf
Sodom will blossom
Gomorrha will be radiant.

Übung

Trauer, mein Text,
ich habe dich gelernt.
Ich zelebriere dich
wieder und wieder
durch die Zeitalter,
die uns mit Maßen
gegeben sind.

Trauer, mein Text,
ich übe dich täglich.
Ich weiß dich
selbst noch im Schlaf.
Sieh nur,
wie fröhlich ich bin.

Exercise

Sorrow, my text,
I have learnt you.
I celebrate you
again and again
through the ages
which are given to us
in moderation.

Sorrow, my text,
I rehearse you daily.
I know you
even in my sleep.
Look
how happy I am.

Reminiszenz

Les ich von Kutschen vorm Tor
von Balken und Truhen im Haus
erscheint mir-
gewichtig drängt er sich auf
und zur Fensterbank hin
blau ist er, bleich, und wie krank-
es dämmert ins Dunkel
geometrisch springt das Gefunkel
im heißen Kamin-
mit Pfefferminz und Jasmin
drängt er sich auf
der Krug
den der Krieg zerschlug.

Reminiscence

When I read of carriages outside the gate
of rafters and wooden chests in the house
it appears to me —
weighty, it forces its way in
and onto the windowsill
it is blue, pale, as though ill —
dusk falls in the dark
geometrically the spark
leaps in the heat of the flame —
with peppermint and jasmine
it forces its way in
the jug
that the war broke.

Alte Kommode

Wenn ich betrachte
die Sträuße, Bänder und Briefe
die Bettchen und Stühlchen
den Schattenriß
dieses Stirb oder Friß
das vereinzelte Wüstenzelt
dies bißchen Welt.
Die Wälder, wo es geschieht.
Eine Tat, eine zweite, die dritte.
Unkenntlich, zu Staub zerfallen
die Bitte —

dann weiß ich, es bleibt
die verschlossene Tür
und das Weiß im Gefieder des Raben.

Neuer Tag

Auferstanden vom Schlaf
gesättigt vom Traum
sind wir da
und fordern den Tag.

Schöneres kann uns nicht blühn
als der Baum vor dem Hause
des Nachbarn.
Begabter können die Sinne nicht sein
als wahrzunehmen
was uns gebührt.

Old Chest of Drawers

When I look at
the nosegays, ribbons and letters
the little beds and chairs
the silhouette
this Die or Do
the solitary desert tent
this little bit of world.
The woods where it happens.
A deed, a second, the third.
Unrecognisable, crumbled to dust
the plea —

then I know what remains is
the locked door
and the white in the raven's plumage.

New Day

Resurrected from sleep
sated by the dream
we are here
and demand the day.

Nothing lovelier can be in store for us
than the tree in flower
outside the neighbour's house.
No senses can be more gifted
than those that perceive
what is our due.

Kleines Japanisches Bild

Ein Himmelssaum
Ein Rosenbaum
Ein seidner Hirt
Ein Weg der ferner wird
Ein nimmermüdes Gras
Unter uns
Und über uns.

Portrait einer Herzogin
überlebensgross
in Purpur gekleidet
im Schloss von T.

Schöner wäre, ihre Hand ließe
den Saum des Mantels fallen
auf Holz, wenn sie schreitet
auf Gras, wenn sie ruht
auf Schnee, wenn sie friert.

Der Maler aber ist schon
gegangen.

Small Japanese Picture

A hem of sky
A rose tree
A silken shepherd
A path leading away
And untiring grass
beneath us
and above us

Portrait of a Duchess
Larger than Life
Dressed in Scarlet
in the Castle of T.

It would be lovelier if her hand
dropped the hem of her coat
on wood when she strides
on grass when she rests
on snow when she is cold.

But the painter has already
left.

Buddha. Eine Begegnung

Jüngling. 18. Jahrhundert.
Alabastern, ein Holzkleid darüber.
Feines abblätterndes Gold. Lotrecht
fallende Arme und Hände. Sehr schlank.
In vollkommenem Stillstand. Bis zur Schulter
reichend. Die Bedeckung des Kopfes perlmuttverziert.
Objekt, Kunstobjekt, eine Art Wiedergeburt.
Schlaflos, resistent gegen Mondschein.
Und lächelnd, mit der dem Wuchs
des erleuchtenden Baumes entsprechenden
Vollendung.

Nur keine Rührung. Es könnte den Satzbau
stören.

Später Nachmittag

Des Sommers müde
ruht ohne Störung
bis fern
teilnehmend am Horizont
diesem Fußpfad hinüber
der See
und lädt ein
übers Wasser zu gehn.

Buddha. An Encounter

A youth. 18th century.
Alabaster, encased in wood.
Thin layer of gold leaf, flaking off.
Arms and bands in vertical fall. Very slim.
In a state of perfect stillness. Reaching
up to the shoulder. The head-dress decorated
with mother-of-pearl.
Object, objet d'art, a type of reincarnation.
Sleepless, impervious to the moonlight.
And smiling with the perfection
that matches the growth
of the illuminating tree.

No sentimentality please. It might upset
the syntax.

Late Afternoon

Tired of summer
tranquil
as far as the eye can see
partaking in the horizon
this footpath across
the lake rests
and beckons you
to walk over the water.

Romanbeginn bei K.

Nicht Calderon traf gegen Mittag
in Rotterdam ein
der andere wars
im schäbigen Mantel
darinnen der Stadtplan
um später ins Kino zu gehen
in die künstliche Sonne.

Ich sehe durchs Stadttor
und verweile ohne Erbarmen
mit meinen Süchten
fern.

Training

Auch das Schreiben will geübt sein,
Schönschrift, langsam, auf und ab.
Linientreu und dunkel sei das Wort,
damit sichs abhebt von
dem bleichen Blatt Papier.

Und so schreibe ich am Morgen
noch geblendet von der Nacht.
Und so schreibe ich am Abend
noch verfinstert von dem Tag,
der sich nicht besinnen mag,
beides je gesehn zu haben.

Beginning of a Novel by K.

It wasn't Calderon who arrived in Rotterdam
towards noon
it was the other
in the shabby overcoat
with a map of the city in his pocket
in order to go to the cinema later
the artificial sun.

I peer through the city gate
and without mercy
I stay away
with my addictions

Training

Even handwriting must be practised,
copybook script, slow, up and down.
Let the word toe the line and be dark,
so it will stand out on
the pale sheet of paper.
And thus I write in the morning
still dazzled by the night.
And thus I write in the evening
still darkened by the day
that doesn't want to recall
ever having seen either.

Nachtgeschichte

Ich bediene mich der Nacht
und wache,
daß der Dieb nicht kommt.
Werde nicht müde,
den Park zu durchschreiten,
das Schattenreich,
das Reich des marmornen Glanzes.

Es wiegen sich Laub und Gras.
Es schmiegt sich der Wind an den See.
Weißgekleidet stehn die Träume da.

Da springt die Glocke aus dem Turm
mit Hieb und Stich
und Schlag auf Schlag
ein Peitschenwerk aus Schlägen.

Night Story

I make use of the night
and keep watch
so the thief won't come
Never tire
of striding through the park,
the kingdom of shadows,
the domain of marble radiance.

Leaves and grass sway.
The wind nestles against the lake.
Dreams stand dressed in white.

All at once the bell springs from the tower
with cut and thrust
and stroke after stroke
a whipwork of strokes.

Zuversicht

Erst kürzlich hörten wir
das Erwachen eines Zweigs,
den Flug der nesterbauenden Vögel,
das Geräusch der sich am Morgen
öffnendenWege des Parks.

Sehen wir nicht himmelwärts
ein sich verschärfendes Blau,
die Blinkzeichen Gestern und Morgen.

Hören wir nicht den Pfiff der Empörung,
einen Hauch von Liebe,
ein uraltes Wort.

Trust

Only recently we heard
the awakening of a branch,
the flight of nest-building birds,
the sound of the park's footpaths
opening up in the moming.

Do we not see skywards
a deepening blue,
the warning lights yesterday and tomorrow.

Do we not hear the whistle of indignation,
a breath of love,
an ancient word.

Vom Morgen zum Abend

Am Morgen
lerne ich zunächst
das Kapitel vom Hören und Sehen.
Dann das Kapitel vom Nehmen und Geben.
Danach das Kapitel vom Hungern und Dürsten.
Und schließlich das Kapitel
vom Lesen und Schreiben.

Ich kontrolliere den Stand der Wörter,
notiere Verlust und Gewinn,
Überfluß und Bedürfnis.
Ich bin in Erwartung.
Erwarte Nie Da Gewesenes.
(Erst gestern entdeckte ich
in einem Gedicht »ein Flugzeug
aus Mann und Frau«.)

Am Abend rekapituliere ich
das Abnehmen der Kräfte
und die Lektion der alten Meister,
nicht oft genug könne die Sonne aufgehen,
und *purpurn* sei sie zu nennen.
Königlicher Mantel
aus Arm und Reich.

From Morning till Night

First thing in the morning
I study the chapter
on hearing and seeing.
Then the chapter on taking and giving.
Then the chapter on hunger and thirst.
And finally the chapter
on reading and writing.

I check the state of the words,
note loss and gain,
surplus and demand.
I arn full of expectation.
Expect the Unheard-Of.
(Just yesterday I discovered
in a poem "an airplane
made of man and woman".)

In the evening I recapitulate
the dwindling of energies
and the old masters' lesson
that the sun can't rise often enough
and is to be called *scarlet*.
Royal cloak
made of poor and rich.

Verzichtsbewusstsein

Lange nicht mehr
die Grenze überschritten
in die Zonen der Bewohnbarkeit
hinein ins knietiefe Gras
ins hüfthohe Korn
in die ansteigende Flut der Gärten.

Lange nicht mehr
im Katzbach ertrunken mit Mann und mit Maus
in der lange verschmähten Kindheit.

Lange nicht mehr
auf der anderen Seite gewesen
im grünlos nackten Gebirg
in den blauen Stadien des Lavendelfelds.

Oder im Blautopf
wo sich das sagenhaft Dunkle verdichtet zu Licht.
In einer seither nicht mehr vorhanden gewesenen
Fremdsprache, ins Schattige führend wie Anästhesie.

Lange kein Gedicht mehr geschrieben.
Arme Gegend, nichts zu holen.
Lange nicht mehr.
Auch nicht auf die Manschetten des Wladimir M.

Awareness of Abdication

Not to have crossed
the boundary into zones that are habitable
in a long time
into knee-high grass
into thigh-deep wheat
into the rising flood of gardens.

Not to have drowned
in the Katzbach river with man and mouse
in the childhood long since spurned.

Not to have been
on the other side in a long time
in the greenless naked mountain ranges
in the blue stages of the lavender field.

Or in the Blue Pond
where the fabled darkness condenses to light.
In a foreign language lost since then
leading to shadowy terrains like anaesthesia.

Not to have written a poem
in a long time.
Barren area, nothing to be got there.
Not in a long time.
Not even on the cuff links of Vladimir M.

Oder auf Albertis vom Meer geglättete Seiten.
Oder unter Hikmets Apfelbaum.

Auch nicht in Staub zu Freunden und Feinden
Oder in Sand, wo unsre Häuser stehn
Oder in Wind, der mir am Kopfe pfiff
Oder ins Jammertal
Oder auf den Himmelsstrich.
Oder auf die Schwelle der Erschrockenheit
auf Papier, Dokument des Standesunterschieds.

Selbst auf die Tafel, schwarz und aus Schiefer
habe ich lange kein Gedicht mehr geschrieben.
Erst kürzlich wurde das letzte gelöscht.
Es stand einsam
seit Generationen.

Or on Alberti's pages smoothened by the sea.
Or beneath Hikmet's appletree.

Nor in dust to friends and foes.
Or in sand where our houses stand
Or in wind that whistled past my head
Or in the valley of tears
Or on the firmament.
Or on the threshold of dread
on paper, token of difference in rank.

Even on the board, black and made of slate
have I not written a poem in a long time
Just recently the last was wiped away.
It stood there all alone
For generations.

Heiliger Januar
(20. 1.1993)

Die am Wege steht
Heilige Sainte-Victoire
leih uns was du bist
für nur diesen Tag

Heilige Rhone in der sich spiegelt
heiliges Blau worin das Wölkchen versickert
über den Häusern mit heilig geschlossenen Läden

Orkus in den wir hinabschauen
Heiliges Hinab
Und das Meer liegt im silbernen Pelz

Mimose Mandel Lavendel
Heiligtümer
Und dein Gesicht liebe Freundin
uns testamentarisch vermacht
sich entfernend
wie zwei Hände voll Wassers
hell und eben geschöpft

Holy January
(20/1/93)

The one by the roadside
Holy Sainte-Victoire
lend us what you are
for just this day

Holy Rhone which mirrors
holy blue wherein the small cloud trickles away
above the houses with holy closed shutters

Orcus we gaze down into
Holy descent
And the sea lies in a silver pelt

Mimosa almond lavender
Holy shrines
And your face dear friend
a legacy bequeathed to us
moving away
like two hands brimful
with bright and freshly drawn water

Nerudas Blau

Das Blau war außer sich vor Freude
Als wir geboren wurden.
Denn zuerst war das Licht
Dann folgte das Blau
Dann folgte der Mensch
Und das Blau erfand ein paar Maler
Und dann und wann einen Dichter dazu

Neruda's blue

The blue was beside itself with joy
When we were born.
For first there was light
Then followed the blue
Then followed man
And the blue invented a few painters
And now and then a poet as well.

Alte Bekannte, von gegenüber

Einige Male sah ich sie am Arm
einer jungen fröhlichen Frau

Blond und gelockt das Haar
Die Absätze zu hoch für den bedürftigen Gang

Dann sah ich sie auf ihrem Balkon
die Straße hinauf und hinab schauend
Wer denn wohl käme

Dann sah ich sie ungesichert den Schritt
zurück in ihr Zimmer tun

Dann sah ich sie herüberschaun
und ich winkte. Sie winkte nicht

All die Monate sah ich nach ihr
im Frühling Sommer Herbst und Winter

In dieser Nacht ist sie geholt worden
Aufrecht wie gekrönt auf geradem Stuhl

der sie trug im weißen Hemd
schmal sehr schmal

eingeschoben in den Rettungswagen
Mit stillem Blaulicht fuhren sie davon

Old acquaintance, from across the street

A few times I saw her on the arm
of a young cheerful woman

Her hair blond and curled
Too high the heels for her tottering walk

Then I saw her on her balcony
gazing up and down the street
To see who might be coming

Then I saw her take a precarious step
back into her room

Then I saw her look across
and I waved. She didn't wave

All those months I looked out for her
spring, summer, autumn and winter

Tonight they collected her
straight as royalty on an upright chair

which carried her in her white nightshirt
slight very slight

They pushed her into the ambulance
Drove away with hushed sirens

WAS IST die Antwort
Was ist die Frage
Auf eine kleine Stele
(9 cm hoch) von Robert Stern

Zwischen Rat und Unrat
Umweg und Weg
Satz und Gegensatz
schwer auf leichtem Fuß
sich nach oben erweiternd
im umgekehrten Pyramidenmaß
herausgeschlagen aus dem Land der Stille
wo Pharaonen ruhn
die Speise im goldenen Gefäß
jahrtausendelang

Rost dämmert herauf
und das Kind aus Kindertagen verzweigt sich gänzlich
in poetischer Mathematik

WHAT IS the answer
What is the question
On a little stela
(9cm high) by Robert Stern

Between advice and vice
bypath and path
thesis and anti thesis
heavy on light foot
widening towards the top
a reversed pyramid
hacked out of the land of stillness
where pharaohs rest
provisions in golden vessels
for thousands of years

rust is dawning
and the child of childhood days ramifies fully
in poetic mathematics

Wohnungen

Die Seele meiner Mutter wohnt in einer Amsel
Die Seele meines Vaters wohnt in einer Abendsonne
Albert wohnt in einem Pfifferling
Ludwig in einem Stellwerk
Hubert in einem Schulheft

Alles kehrt wieder
und ist schon zu Ende.

Daß ihr erfahrt wie es um mich bestellt ist

Ich wehre den Hochhäusern in denen wir uns spiegeln
der Himmel und ich.
Ich verwerfe das herrische Gezirp in den Bäumen der Vögel,
den Winter die Gruften
die Berühmtheiten
die reinseidenen Mäntel
und bitte die Heiligen Buchstaben
mein Leben zu verlängern.

Was wiederholt geschehen ist.

Dwellings

My mother's soul dwells in a blackbird
My father's soul dwells in an evening sun
Albert dwells in achanterelle
Ludwig in a signal box
Hubert in an exercise book
Everything returns
and is already at an end.

In order that you learn how I am faring

I wage war against the skyscrapers in which we are mirrored
the sky and myself.
I reject the bossy twitter in the trees of birds,
the winter the tombs
the celebrities
the coats of pure silk
and ask the Holy Letters
to prolong my life.

As has repeatedly occurred.

Familiengrab

Ein Stenogramm für David Jakob

Liegt Einer einen Kieselstein
in die rechte untere Ecke
der marmornen Platte aufs Grab.

Liegt Einer geboren/gestorben
eim Leben gelebt Arbeit und Liebe
vielfach gescheitert.
Als würde dies alles
dereinst
wiedergutgemacht
auch die Irrtümer der Erde
auch die Schmerzen
die da kreisen gedankenverloren
im immer krummer werdenden Körper.

Wieviel wiegt eine Rose in Rot
Wie viel ein Stein aberwitzig leicht wie
der Vogel die Feder das Auge der Punkt

Family Grave

A message in shorthand for David Jakob

There's One who places a pebble
in the lower right-hand corner
of the marble slab on the grave.

There's One who lies born/ dead
lived a life work and love
failed in a variety of ways.
As though all this would
one day
be put right
also the errors of the earth
also the pains
which circulate lost in thought
in the increasingly hunched body.

How much does a rose weigh in red
How much a stone absurdly light as
the bird the feather the eye the full stop

Zweifel

Die Berge hüllen sich in Schweigen
Der Schnee verbirgt das Leuchten
Der Fischer schiebt das Boot den Fischen zu
Jenseits der Wolken
Vielleicht
Das Licht

Märchen

Auf der Suche
nach etwas Schönem wie Schnee
ging ich leer aus
bis es des Wegs zu schneien begann

Doubt

The mountains shroud themselves in silence
The snow conceals the radiance
The fisherman pushes the boat towards the fishes
Beyond the clouds
Perhaps
The light

Fairy Tale

On the look-out
for something beautiful like snow
I came away empty-handed
till it began to snow on my path

Heimat - eine Leuchtschrift

Eine jener Schriften deren wir bedürfen
Wo denn nun wo
Zwischen Orion und Eos
460 pc im Nebel entfernt und verloren

Hier unten vielleicht
wo die Knochen verwehn
oder ruhn
Zwischen dem einen schon vergessenen Schmerz
Und dem zukünftigen
Dem schrillen Ton nach Mitternacht
wenn sich der Traum unterbricht

Heimat ist wo wir waren
oder sein werden ist nicht Krieg
wo der Knopf an der Jacke nicht fehlt
wo die Suppe noch warm ist

Heimat ist ein kurzer Satz
ein langer Satz ein Vers
ein Wort ein Amen

Home - a luminous script

One of those scripts we have need of
Where is it where
Between Orion and Eos
460 parsec away and lost in a nebula

Down here perhaps
where the bones scatter to the winds
or lie at rest
Between the already forgotten pain
and the future one
The shrill sound after midnight
when the dream interrupts itself

Home is where we were
or will be is not war
where the button isn't missing from the jacket
where the soup is still warm

Home is a short sentence
a long sentence a verse
a word an amen

Eines Tages

Eines Tages stand ich am Ufer des Mississippi.
(Keine Erzählung.)
Das Hochwasser führte in dem ihm eigenen,
beschleunigten Fließen
mit sich 1 gedunsene Kuh 1 gedunsenes Schwein
1 gedunsenen Baum 1 gedunsenen Strauch.
Nicht aber den Dampfer mit Rad.

Als ich mich unbeobachtet sah
tauchte ich eine Hand in das Kadaverwasser
meiner Kindheit.
Das ist keine Erzählung.
Das ist der Augenblick.

Frühmorgens der See

Glattgezogen, ein silbernes Laken
Darauf verstreut die Möwen in Weiß
Trümmer Scherben Fetzen
Eines Briefs
Eines überdimensionalen Abschieds

One day

One day I stood on the banks of the Mississippi.
(Not a story)
The flood water carried in its typically accelerated flow
1 bloated cow 1 bloated pig
1 bloated tree 1 bloated shrub.
Not however the steamer with wheel.
Seeing myself unobserved
I dipped my hand into the cadaverous water
of my childhood.
This is not a story.
This is the moment.

The lake in the early morning

Stretched smooth, a silver sheet
Scattered all over with seagulls in white
Ruins fragments shreds
Of a letter
Of a parting large beyond measure

Gedicht für den Anfang

I

Gedichte sollen geschrieben werden
für euch
eigens für euch
weil ihr so jung seid
und wichtig.
Schon wieder eine neue Generation.

Gedichte für den Aufbruch und Ausbruch
weil ihr noch jung seid.
Noch seid ihr sehr jung.

Gedichte
die zeigen, worauf es ankommt.
Gemeint ist das Leben
mit Frage und Antwort darauf.

Aber das weiß ich nicht,
weiß es nicht mehr.
Und alles ist anders.
Seht euch doch um.
Und vergleicht es mit mir.
Doch wozu.

Poem for the beginning

1

Poems should be written
for you
especially for you
because you are so young
and important.
Once more a new generation.

Poems to set out and break out with
because you are still young.
You're still very young.

Poems
that show what matters.
By this I mean life
and its questions and answers.

But that I don't know,
don't know it any longer.
And everything's changed.
Just look around you.
And compare it with me.
But what for.

2

Drei Dinge noch seien gesagt:
Zum ersten gibt's schon Gedichte
die müßt ihr euch finden zum zweiten
zum dritten schreibt sie euch selbst.
Wenn es hart auf hart kommt.
So kommt's.
Und ihr mal allein seid.
Das kommt.

Und dann kommt rüber
es dauert nicht lang.
Das wird eine Freude.

2

Three more things should be said:
Firstly there are poems already
secondly you must find them
and thirdly write them yourselves.
When things get rough.
Which they will.
And you're alone.
Which you will be.

And then come over
it won't take long.
What a joy it will be.

Für Maximilian am ersten Schultag

Du gehst, Sechsjähriger,
mit den ernstzunehmenden Büchern
des Beginns auf dem Rücken
um Neues zu lernen

das ABC das Einmaleins
von vielen Geboten: zehn
So fängt es an wie es schon einmal angefangen hat
um immer weiter zu gehn
um zu steigen hoch und höher hinauf
wie ein federleichter wunderlicher Drache
wirst du uns vorkommen der aus ist aufs Steigen bedacht
ist aufs Fallen
getrieben von den unterschiedlichen Sonnen und Monden –
von Sternzeichen zu Sternzeichen
von System zu System
von A zu O
von den Freuden der Berge
den Mühen der Täler
von Mensch zu Mensch
Wir wünschen dir Reise und Rückkehr.

For Maximilian on his first day of school

There you go, six-year-old,
with the weighty books
of the beginning on your back
to learn new things

the ABC the multiplication tables
of many commandments: ten
And so it begins as it began before
in order to go on and on
to climb high and higher
like a kite wondrous and light as a feather
you will seem to us set on rising intent
on falling
driven by the diverse suns and moons
from star sign to star sign
from system to system
from A to O
from the joys of the mountains
the labours of the valleys
from human to human
We wish you voyage and return.

Zimmer 48

Ich harre aus
bis der Regen nachläßt
bis der Abend kommt
bis es an die Tür klopft
und eintritt der Engel
mit seinem Gefolge

Ich harre aus
bis die Gedichte von Rózewicz gelesen sind
und ich wieder weiß
ohne Liebe ist auch das Gedicht
vergeblich

Room 48

I abide
until the rain ceases
until evening comes
until there's a knock on the door
and the angel enters
with his entourage

I abide
until the poems by Rózewicz are read
and I know once more
without love even the poem
is in vain.

Singsang

so daß ich weiß
wohin mich am Ende
die Reise führt
diese lange Reise zum Ende hin
zu diesem Ende das mir
vorausgesagt ist

so daß ich weiß
was mir bevorsteht
ein Garten ohne Bank
ein Baum ohne Schatten
ohne Hunger und Durst
und ohne die flügelweiten Wünsche

so daß ich weiß
nicht eines trägt
kein Rockabye
kein langsamer Singsang
Komm bring mir die Ruh.

Singsong

so that I know
where in the end
this journey will take me
this long journey towards the end
towards this end that was
foretold me

so that I know
what will await me
a garden without a bench
a tree without shade
without hunger and thirst,
and without the wishes wide as wings

so that I know
that no thing will carry
no rockabye
no slow singsong
Come bring me rest

Ein paar Dichter

Nach der Lektüre von Gedichten
in einer literarischen Zeitschrift

Der Damalige

Er ist wieder da.
Ein Rückfall in die Begabung
von gestern
und schreibt ein Gedicht.
Ich horche
nicht mehr wie damals
als uns die Jugend zunichte machte
und groß.

Der Alltägliche

Er kennt keine Blockaden.
Auch die Rasur ist ein Thema,
das Blut leuchtet
wie Woyzeck dem Büchner.
Nur schreibend bist du ein Dichter
nur so.
Mit einem Kopf der dich trennt
von dir und den anderen
im Schwindel
der die Stufe als Abgrund erkennt
daß dich schaudert.

A Few Poets

After reading poems
in a literary magazine

The Poet of Yesterday

He is back again.
A throwback to the talent
of yesterday
and writes a poem.
I don't listen
as I used to in those days
when youth destroyed us
and made us great.

The Poet of the Everyday

He knows no writer's block.
Even shaving is a topic,
the blood shines
like Woyzeck
shone for Büchner.
You're a poet
only when you write,
only then.
With a head separating you
from yourself and the others
at the dizzy moment
when you realize the step
is the abyss
and you shiver.

Der Schweigsame

Kein Wort gelingt, schreibt er,
kein Wort.
Und schreibt und schreibt.
Das Schweigen, schreibt er,
ohne Antrieb, Zeit noch Gegenwart
und schreibt
daß es die Seiten schwärzt
bis zur Unlesbarkeit.
Du schöne Kunst,
bewundernd halt ich ein.

The Poet of Silence

No word succeeds, he writes
No word.
And writes and writes.
The silence, he writes,
without inner drive, time nor present
and writes
till the pages turn black
till they're illegible.
Oh beautiful art,
admiringly I come to a halt.

Der Hirtenknabe von Lenbach

1

Mein Bild, das nie mir gehörte,
hing im Studierzimmer meines Onkels
unweit des leicht angehobenen Kopfteils
einer Liege zu Ruhezwecken,
so daß sich der Ruhende
ein Bild machen mußte.

Während der Onkel studierte
betrachtete ich liegend
die schmutzigen Füße des Knaben
auch die unordentliche Kleidung
mit Befremden
und mein reinliches Kleid.
Ich prüfte die unbewegliche Hand
über den Augen.
Darüber wurde es blau
und ich fürchtete mich.

2

Nach Jahrzehnten sehe ich ihn wieder.
Das war gestern, unerwartet,
das blieb von einem alten Pfarrhaus,
überm Kirschbaumsekretär.

Der Knabe heil ganz ohne Riß.
Der Knabe der da hat gesiegt.
Der Knabe überlebt.

Und über ihm und immer noch
der antwortlos vom Blau
verstellte Himmel.

The Young Shepherd by Lenbach

1
My painting that was never mine
hung in my uncle's study
near the slightly raised head rest
of a chaise longue,
so that whoever reclined there
had to take note of it.

While my uncle worked
I lay and regarded
the boy's dirty feet
and untidy clothes
with displeasure
then my clean dress.
I examined his motionless hand
resting on his eyes.
Above it everything turned blue
and I was afraid.

2
Decades later I see him again.
It was yesterday, unexpected,
relic from an old vicarage
over the cherry-wood desk.

The boy intact without a scratch.
That boy there was triumphant.
That boy survives.

And above him and answerless
as ever the sky
disguised by blue.

Der Tod eines Mädchens

Infarkt, Thrombose, Embolie,
welche Worte
für ein Mädchen schmal
wie ein Kind und wie neu.

Ruh dich aus
oder willst du hinaus?
Es will Abend werden und Frühling.
Die Stadt ist weit und eng.
In den Kolonnaden hängen
die bläulichen Wolken
betriebsamer Autos.
Das sticht in die Schläfen
ein wenig und fein.
Der Scirocco ergreift dir
das Herz.
Kommst du hinaus
oder bist du zu müd
und willst sterben.
Dann bleib ich, bleib ich
bei dir.

Death of a Girl

Heart attack, thrombosis, embolism
such words
for a girl slim
as a child and as new.

Rest a little
or do you want to go out?
Evening is coming and spring.
The city is vast and narrow.
Grey-blue clouds
of busy cars
gather in the arcades.
A stinging in the temples
fine as a needle.
The scirocco grabs hold
of your heart.
Come on out
or are you too tired
and want to die.
I'll stay then, I'll stay
with you.

Reden wir nicht mehr von Landschaft.
Reden wir vom fein kalkulierten Netz
der Längen- und Breitengrade
von den bläulichen Ozeanen
und den hellen Flecken der Kontinente.
Reden wir von den berührbaren Polen
einer sanft rotierenden Kugel
von der gefahrlosen Dürre der Wüsten
dem verläßlichen Grün der Wildnisse
dem Geraschel von Tier und Mensch
und von den punktgenauen Städten.
Betreten wir demnächst und entledigt
die Milchstraße. Der Ausweg
für die unbelehrbaren Metaphern

Let's not talk about landscape any longer.
Let' s talk about the precise network
of longitudes and latitudes
about the oceans' shimmering blue
and the bright spots of continents.
Let's talk about tangible poles
of a gently rotating ball
about the harmless drought of the deserts
the reliable green of the wilderness
the rustling of beast and man
and the accuracy of cities.
Let us stride out soon and with relief
on the milky way, escape route
for all the recalcitrant metaphors.

Alter Jüdischer Friedhof im Mai

Wer lebt hier
Ich höre vereinzelt Gesang .
und den Sprung des Eichhorns hinab.

Wer ist hier der Herr
Aufrecht horchen die Steine.

Wer wirft das Kleid
Es fällt der Schatten von Bäumen
Es fällt das Licht aus der Hand.

Wer geht durch das Gras
Sieh doch. Die Stille.

Old Jewish Cemetery in May

Who lives here
Now and then I hear singing
and the squirrel's downward leap.

Who is the master here
Upright, the stones listen.

Who throws the dress
The shadow falls from trees
The light falls from the hand.

Who walks through the grass
Look! The silence.

Verweigerung der Aussage

Später, viel später
wenn der Täter alt geworden ist
und das Opfer vergeßlich
wie ein Sieb

werde ich mich
zu erinnern suchen
und fluchen weil
das Gedächtnis nichts hält.

Später, viel später
werde ich zu Protokoll geben
was ich nicht weiß

Refusal to give Testimony

Later, much later
when the perpetrator has grown old
and the victim forgetful as a sieve
I'll try
to remember
and curse because
my memory holds nothing.

Later, much later,
I will put on record
what I don't know.

The Dedalus Press Poetry Europe Series:

1: **Sorgegondolen** : *The Sorrow Gondola*
Tomas Tranströmer : (Sweden) translated by *Robin Fulton*

2: **Dingfest** : *Thingsure*
Ernst Jandl : (Austria) translated by *Michael Hamburger*

3: **Aux Banquets du Diable** : *At the Devil's Banquets*
Anise Koltz : (Luxembourg) translated by *John F. Deane*

4: **L'Homme et ses Masques** : *Man and his Masks*
Jean Orizet : (France) translated by *Pat Boran*

5: **Libretto** : *Libretto*
Edoardo Sanguineti : (Italy) translated by *Pádraig J. Daly*

6: **Stances perdues** : *Lost Quatrains*
Alain Bosquet : (France) translated by *Roger Little*

7: **A Tenenat Here**: Selected Poems
Pentti Holappa : (Finland) translated by *Herbert Lomas*

8: **Ljus av ljus** : *Light From Light*
Ingemar Leckius : (Sweden) translated by *John F. Deane*

9: **Sommerfugledalen** : *Butterfly Valley*
Inger Christensen : (Denmark) translated by *Susanna Nied*

10: **Bercée au vent du Nord** : *Rocking to the North Wind*
Liliane Wouters : (Belgium) translated by *Anne-Marie Glasheen*

11: **Diván del Tamarit** : *The Tamarit Poems*
Federico García Lorca : (Spain) translated by *Michael Smith*

12: **Winter auf weissem Blatt** : *Winter on White Paper*
Elisabeth Borchers : (Germany) translated by *Eva Bourke*